Smoke

Poems of love, longing and ecstasy

Ayesha K. Faines

ISBN-13: 978-0692615768 (Kamil Publishing)
ISBN-10: 0692615768

For those who love my darkness and my light.

Contents

Vibrations on a Hardwood Floor

He told me his fingers could get trapped in my roots
and he wasn't speaking of my family tree.
I was his sugar rum cherry
syrupy treat
and so bitter sweet.
He said I spoke in verse
and giggled in rhyme.
He said I reminded him of a tune
too elusive to recall.
My body was inspiration
impossible to transcribe
so he made a point to
commit me
in all my dimensions
to memory.
Incre((mentally))
he became trapped in these roots
just as I feared.
I was his a-
His a(hhh)
His af(firmation)
His Afr(ica)
His afro,
Afro-disiac.

Damn.

Smoke

I.
Dark: Silhouette
classical form
leans over the city
like he is King.

Finale
to our making
love.

A serpent coils
to Damascene beat

sputters over a city street.

Swirl and sputter.
Writhe and coil.

Black serpent to the night.

II.
I lean in for a light.

Join him in the fire

escape.
Loose limbed
lonely feeling
brave.

I want him to speak to me
as if I were the air

hold me close
rest his nose in my hair.

But he only kicks it
with the night.

So we wish upon buildings
and blow out the lights.

III.
Against the howling city life
as panthers clawed the
flesh of night

he taught me to smoke.

To balance the cig between
locked lips,

squeeze my cheeks
cock my hip
raise my chin
like I'm too proud
and blow sweet kisses
toward the clouds.

Slow sultry drags
of smoke wrapped
my hair
in tempest brew
tornadoes tangoed
smoke bombs blew
ripped open their blouses
as if too tight and
shook their breasts
with great delight.

IV.
Beautiful
bound in silver sashes
moon on our shoulders
stars in our lashes

We wrote love letters
and watched them

fall

    with

        the

            ashes.

Smoked in a language
fascinating and new.
Spoke things taboo.
We undid syntax
stripped it down
threw out verbs and nouns.
Distilled a language
that could only exist between
a mighty roar
and a parting kiss.

V.

He taught me to smoke.
He taught me to smolder.
How to glow hot
and to turn a cold shoulder.

To dance behind veils
to tempt
and demand
that sex and silence

go hand in hand.

He taught me how to let go
to kill the flame
and let the wind take care
of any remains

as if they were love.

Seminal

New York, New York

light
>	on my cheek
I close my eyes
see
>	the sun
sliding in the thighs of dawn
burning a new day into being

I dream of
>	constellations
and the night we
danced a galaxy
>	into beating

I dream of
>	libations
poured just as moon
reached her perigee

I dream of
>	those things we could not retrieve:

seconds

beneath the mattress

words in a glass

echoes gathered

between   palm and skin

Newport, Rhode Island

I awake

to a profusion of gold

leaves falling like aged grapes

into a mouth of crooked tombs

There is life and death

In my reflection   Both coexisting

                 Both feeling like freedom

Apocalyptic Madness

Because the world could be ending
and the earth is trembling
and we're buying time
on credit cards and loans

let's love.

We haven't anytime to waste.
This is a matter of right
and now,
as the moments
and the minutes
and the hours
wind down

I need for you to be down
with loving me

like this is your last opportunity

to walk toward eternity
to make time spin

even if we are close to the end

let's love.

Because we all can hear the vibrations
of flat lines breaking
and ancient mosques are vacant

lets fall on our knees praying
that peace will come our way
as we approach our final day

and let's love.

Let us prune a friendship
entwine the limbs of our family tree
in 24 hours time

because the numbers are draining
and sisters are complaining
that love stopped loving me.

So brother, I need you, in this instance,
to not be so picky

and let's love.

Let's procreate
before it gets too late.

Because the man at the station
is preaching revelations
and his Kangol hat has a few dollars
and very little cents

let's love.

Because the Levant is in flames
and democracy in vain
and leaders are chain smoking
in an opium den

let's love.

Because a Black Prince has come
and hope was spun
into an American dream
then all that shit Nostradamus said
must be

so baby

let's love.

And because history has been discovered
and new stuff
uncovered
that isn't really new at all,
because cities are sinking
and empires
rise
and fall

let's love.

If the calendar days are scarce
and holidays are false
let's make a holy day of our own.

We don't need a preacher
Or justice of the peace.

You don't even have to marry me.

Now you know I'm tripping

As mothers mourn
and racists sink tea,

let's love.

Look at me.
Hear me.

Love is the only gladness
amidst this apocalyptic madness,
the only thing that makes sense
our only glimpse of
peace.

And because the world could be
ending

let's love.

Greed

That time I fed you
my fingers
and you said they tasted like
honey
wine and salt.

Déjà Vu

I loved you once
on a Corsican street
near rustic storefronts and casks of wine.
In shanty towns and empyrean isles,
my love for you has spread for miles.

I loved you once
over maté flasks
'neath a champagne moon
on shards of glass.
In Nantucket,
in a whicker chair,
I loved you in the salt-cured air.

I loved you here.
I loved you there.

I loved you
on a celestial plane,
in childhood dreams,
in dazzling rain,
while frolicking
in fields of clover,
I loved you under.

I loved you over.

I loved you in the suede of peaches
in old newspapers,
on foggy beaches
and in a flash of silver slither.

I loved you hither.
I loved you thither.

I loved you in another's bed,
in silent films
inside my head.
In the refrigerator's hum,
in Dombe drums,
I loved *you* in the morning.

I loved you in Cordoban nights,
in discotheques
and swaths of light,
in Chinese gardens,
apothecaries,
eating ripe greengages
and sweet black cherries.

I loved you in vanilla suds,

midnight soaks
in claw foot tubs.
In the over flow,
in wrinkled skin

I love you now.
I loved you then.

I loved you over a Coltrane track.
I loved you sharp.
I loved you flat.
In pages of Baldwin
and Langston verse,
in mosques
in temples
in a Baptist church
I prayed for our love.

I loved you crouched
before cupped hands.
I loved you crossing
Bedouin sands.
I loved you from my window sill
as girls skipped rope
I loved you still.

I loved you.

I loved you through a hurricane.
I loved you suckling sugar cane.
I loved you in my history books,
in oil paintings,
in second looks,
at the brief sight of a comely face,
My, I've loved you all over the place.

I loved you.

I loved you in a quiet madness.
I loved you in an empty gladness.
I loved you at a humming bird's pace.
I loved you with flamingo grace.
Though only once I'd seen your face
I feel I have loved you all my lifetime.

I
loved you
before I knew
you.
Before I knew
that I could
love

you.

Certainly,

I loved you

before you loved

me.

Monday Poem

On Monday
you are everywhere
and nowhere.
You are
in aisle one
by the onions.
You are there.
You are
in my horoscope
near the public fountain
and nowhere.
And when I turn the corner
I see a shadow
lurking over the street,
but you have me beat.

For dinner
I make cinnamon chicken
broccoli raab
with jasmine rice
wondering if that is what you would like
after work
If I was entertaining you
with fragrant banter

behind a kitchen sink.
And no where.

I eat alone.
Turn the tv
wondering if you were here with me
what you'd like to see.
End up on the news.
Remember how all this damn murder
upsets you too
and when I kneel down in prayer
I feel you there.

Sun sets
I soak my feet
red polish my toe nails
sitting on the edge of the tub
wondering, if you were around
would you give me a long back rub?
And no where.
Take off my shirt
unbutton my bra
sharing my glory
with only the walls.
No one else can see this splendor
No one else can feel this surrender

No one else can hear me think incessantly
or see
the world as I do : a deep indigo hue.

And then finally I rest my head
close my eyes
and smile.
There you go.
There you go!
Yes! You've made it!
You've arrived in my dreams
and not a minute too soon.
Time for our midnight rendezvous.

Slumber rescues me
from a
final thought
wondering
if at the end of the day
you're thinking of me
too.

This is my Monday soliloquy.
And still
there's a whole week ahead of me.

Locks

"I feel you."
I nod.
Injera
parts the
doro wat sea.

I just lied.

I want to
feel you

literally.

I should plead
rather than eat

Admit
To being empty.
Aroused
by your discourse,
wanting your words
to roll over
my tongue, wanting

to taste
their source.

Pardon me Mister
but,
the way you speak
of liberation,
lick your lips
and swig Merlot
is distracting
as hell.

Can't you tell?

You have a beautiful mind.
And I have been denied
your strong flavor
of intellect
for far too long.

I have a proposition.

Why don't we
turn my kitchen
into the headquarters
of your mission?

Your private study
could be
the triangle
between my knees
and chest.

At bed time,
you may
inscribe
your vision
in my scarlet depths.

I would burn
incense,
jasmine
and frankincense,
as you meditate to Monk
and maybe some Miles too.
I really dig Bitches Brew.

And I would
be there
to capture
your every brilliant thought

Like honey

from the apiary

I could be a damned good secretary.

I want your locks to
sprawl
on my pillow
sinuous
as algae dancing
on the floor of the
sea

I want to bathe with you
and pray with you
facing the East.
I want you to lay hands
on me
as I sleep
and be affirmed of your walk in life.

 I want to be your
comrade,
confidant
and concubine,
to serve you dates
and mint tea

in a perfume negligee.

Brother,
at the end of the day
let me be your
liberation.

A fierce seduction
would ease your weary imagination.

Let me unclutter that space
between
you and God
until your manifesto flows freely
from your lips,
and you may recite it softly
as you take control of my hips.

I want to be your exemplar
and disciple,
when others are slow to follow
your lead.

Let me be there
to kiss your shoulders
when you craft a plan

to rescue the black man from deception and lies.

I would like to be your woman

because every revolutionary needs a queen
with whom he can co-rule
and dream
and return home to
with the spoils
of war.

Or....
we can just sit here
and continue to be polite
all night.

Believers

For a love that washes fresh,
and stimulates the skin,
that titillates like lilies,
shivering in the wind.

For a love like French vanilla,
that is noble, and sublime
as a waft of Gold Coast jasmine,
that lingers over time.

For a love like swollen raindrops
that ripple into tears.
For a love like lines of laughter
that crease over years.

Like Damascus,
A love that is ancient and spiritual,
For a love like Tunisian twilight
twinkling a Padpadrascha hue.

For a love like the Tower of Babel,
that reaches for the unseen,
that diminishes its lover,
and exalts a Sufi's dream.

For a love like Old World dust,
that swirls through time and space,
revived by swollen raindrops
giving glory
truth and grace.

They wait.

First to Fall

I wasn't ready for you to skip ahead
to read the chapters
I hadn't read.
But you turned my pages
like an open book in wind
and found your life
from beginning to end.

Blues for my Man

(somewhere an imaginary band plays)

I don't wear
a gardenia in my hair
but baby,
I still sing the blues.
So thank you for the heartache,
and a special thanks for my new attitude.

When you first laid eyes on me
you were like Billy Dee!
And I Miss Ross
I swooned for your dizzy charms.
So thank you for that sweet gesture.
Short and sweet
And thank you very much for my song.

How could I ever resist
your honey suckle kiss
tumbling down my bare spine?
You know I loved it when you kissed me there
Baby, thank you for those tears I cried.
And thank you for the bitter wine.

Good morning heartache!

Hear I go again.
Good morning heartache!

Can't no other song spin.

Me and Billie got this thing
and it's more than the swing that I do
when I hear her croon.

I cried for you
 she sings
and baby,
I cry for you.

Finally someone gave me something to pout about,
something to shout about,
something to wail out loud about!

You put the b flat
in my tune.
So thank you for the heartache,
Yes, I thank you for the heartache!
I said, I love you for the heartache!
And a special thanks for my new attitude.

Can't you hear me singing the blues?

All of me

Singing the blues?

Why not take all of me

Singing the blues?

Can't you see

Blue.

I'm no good without you...?

Two Black Breasts

In between my breasts

there is:

Black rain
Black orchids
Black desire

Black light
stalactites
a reservoir of tears.

The ashes of those
who have crossed
this land.

Two dots
and a line

shadows and a sword.

Puddles
embryos
life and death.

Disaster and laughter
and conga beats

and you
attempting to raise a flag.

No More War

I love you
and I'll give up
reason.
I love you
and I'll
surrender right.

Just to have you in my kingdom.

A place bearing
offerings
of silk
cardamom
and gold.
A space
to entertain you
with song
dance
and erotic poetry.
Feed you lavishly
endless spreads
of forbidden fruit.

I welcome your dictatorship

as long as you liberate me
from fear.

Grant me the freedom
to love you
without err.

Defend our borders,
love.
Protect my honor.

You can rule me
as long as you promise
to never end
the tyranny.

Voyage

We lay on the shore
of an Isley sound
water
between each toe
trickled over the torso
at the meeting of thighs.

You returned to Atlantis.

We swam through indolent waves
in rolled cuffs
and cotton dress.
I thought, maybe clouds torn
by Hathor.
But it was your groans
each more urgent than before.
Thrashes of the tongue
rocked and tilted
my neck
sending my chin into air
like a mast.
And at that moment you kissed that part of my throat
that makes me deliver
sweet, salty, sad

laughter.

Atlantis : a queen-sized bed
in a Harlem studio
that overheats in winter.

And you'll always come back to me.

Kissing Kismet

I wasn't tired
until the rumble of his snore
sank deep into the reservoirs of my ears
like lukewarm
St. Maarten sea water.

He drowned me in shallow sleep.
The kind, incapable of shrinking an hour into a short of
twisted fantasy.
I was completely found in the moment.

I wondered,
 how does one make love to a narcissist?
(Trick question)
He keeps love for himself.

Back then,
our wrists were connected with a twisted ribbon,
embroidered on one side,
raw on the other.
And each day,
I never knew if I'd wake choked
in beautiful
or

even more threadbare
than before.

So, I always hoped for beautiful.
And I was happy,
I know this.
Or else I would not have returned for more.

Tonight,
he is enamored with the way the slope of my thigh falls
generously
into the valley of my navel
and his lazy hands
venture on endless excursions,
always starting and ending
at the same point :
my lips.

Finally,
the day arrived
when my body mattered
more than his.
And I didn't know how to rejoice in it.

He had changed.
So had I.

It is the universe,

not people,

that creates relationships,

that controls the horizontal gravity,

more lovingly called kismet,

and like all things operating within this single universal domain,

time

is the hinging factor.

Two lovers can meet at the wrong time and just be friends.

Two friends can meet at the wrong time and just be lovers.

A romance as enduring as a pillar of salt can be a tryst,

if attempted at T minus 2.

Or a tryst

can be a tryst

that was a tryst

and still is a tryst

and will always be a tryst.

Time makes the difference because time is us.

I realize that now as the flippancy with which I am determined to treat this rendezvous is incessantly interrupted with heartfelt confessions, promises

that just may outlast their time in space.

Could we ever love in a way that was untwisted?

Yes.

Theoretically we could make beautiful

if we put our intelligent minds to it,

but maybe

T minus 2

would forever tarnish

our magnificent possibility

with its bitter

(in)difference.

I could only wonder, as his slumbering body sank further into mine.

Some people are worth enjoying. Some people are worth the wait. And some people are not worth your time.

When I Get to Philly

When I get to Philly
I'm going to visit your new place,
I'm going to compliment your linens
and admire your good taste.

When I get to Philly
I'm going to dress up for our date,
I'm going to listen to your stories
and feed you from my plate.

When I get to Philly
you'll still crack corny jokes.
We'll call each other by our nicknames;
I bet we'll laugh until it hurts!

When I get to Philly
it'll be a homecoming for flesh.
You'll prop my right leg on your shoulder
like you never even left.

When I get to Philly
I'm going to rediscover your tattoo
and the way you scrunch your face
so funny, when you're about to come through.

Oh baby, I'm going be so good to you in Philly
and you'll be better than before,
because it's only like you, darlin',
to keep me coming back for more.

We're going to love so hard in Philly,
it will make up for the past
but baby,
when I get to Philly this time,
it has to be the last.

Expiration Date

(Have you ever entertained this thought?)

Does love evaporate
Or experience rebirth?

Are we the mausoleums
housing loves ghosts?

When it leaves
this worldly place
is it scattered over sea?

Or is love expired
occasionally damned to be hate for all eternity?

Because that would explain a lot.

Superman

I find you
in the ashes
in the slithering heat
and constellation of stone.

In a field of ruins
where dust rains
where oil and blood
dance
between cinder blocks
and bone.

This is where you reveal
your super powers,
always in my darkest hours.
You jump pyres
give breath to flesh,
you raise a staff
to part the sea.

This is where we meet:
ground zero,
when I am most in need
of a hero

to pull me from the rubble
and place the clouds
at my feet.

8 AM

Twist! First taste of morning shower.
Suds erase the moonlit hours.
Ahhh! Heat rises, drapes the pain,
while ten o'clock rolls down the drain.
Limbs ascending, bodies blending
earthly rhythm never ending.
Hand prints, sweat and salt lips trace
vanish as water pounds my face.
What I'd give to crown last night
with rapture, love strokes of delight
but fury , such a fleeting flame
returns, like water, from whence it came.

Madness for Two

I want to feed you from my plate.
Watch you savor
swallow
and digest this madness.
Watch it dribble on your chin.

I want to hand you a napkin
to dab the madness
even though there are crumbs in my lap,
and grease on my cheeks.

I want to teach you dining etiquette:
How to be elegant
and mad.
How to chew
and sit erect
and speak
without revealing the madness.

I want to be a lady
and sit across from you
with nothing on my plate
but a sprig of mint
to cleanse my pallet.

And I want to watch

as you indulge in

five courses:

lonely to start.

An intermezzo

of misery

and then glee

hope

despair

and the wine of love

which your waiter will refill

without your knowing.

I want you to drink until your knees

are weak

and judgment blurred.

I want you to ravage delicacies from the desert tray:

marzipan

and candied apples,

things that stick to your teeth

and taste terribly sweet.

I want you to eat

and loosen your suspenders

take off your tie
and shoes
and scoot back in your seat.

And then I'll hand you
a towelette
and send you a way.

Full .
Uncomfortable.
Sloppy.

Grinning.
Satisfied.

I just want to indulge you in the same madness
that indulges me.

Sweet.

Grasping Water

To every love,
a time and place,
a stage, where romance shows
her face.

Catch love by the tails of night
and leave it where you find it.

To every love
a certain gloom,
the Sun will always
cede to Moon.

Catch love by the veil of light
and leave it where you find it.

To every love
a kaleidoscope,
that blurs the blues
and sharpens hope.

Catch love in the blue of green,
and leave it where you find it.

Seek love
if it be in China,
Mozambique,
or Asia Minor,

catch love on the passing train,
but leave it
where you find it.

Excavation

I climb your words
as if they are steps
to an ancient temple.
I dare to go where my breath will be
compromised
by altitude;
my life, by death.
I use your letters to brace myself.
I use your punctuation to stop
and admire the view,
and when I reach the top
I sleep in the spaces
as if they are hidden chambers,
waiting to be
aroused
by your spirit.

Tripping
(Not an ego in sight)

I'm holding on to the memory
of when you were in love with me.
Filled my head with sweet visions,
cooked in my kitchen
rubbed my feet when I came home...

And now the music's gone.

Tell me baby, what did I do wrong?

I cleaned out the attic,
saw us in Paris.
The edges are wrinkled now
but I still make out your smile.
It sure has been a while.

Tell me baby, what you're up to now?

I still can't eat,
I can not sleep
in the bed where you loved me.
The way you kissed my nipples,
the way I would tremble.

Oh come on daddy, now the sugar's gone...
The honey jar is empty
but the kitchen is warm.

If you stop by I'll let you in...
And you can stay for the weekend.

And I'll love you again and
again.

Or maybe we can just play
pretend.

I'd walk a river. I'd paint the sky,
just to have you as my guy.

To have you love me over,
and run my bath water...

I still don't know why you left me.
Doesn't matter, baby, come and rescue me.

Come back big daddy.
You make me happy.

Love Under House Arrest

Who are you to place my love

under house arrest?

Capture it contain

it

like a fire fly to a jar

and flee

leaving me to light the night?

Who are you to place my love

under house arrest?

Conquer it control

it

like a Venus

that longs for the dark entrails of the sea?

Who are you to place my love

under house arrest?

To strike the match

that leaves me glowing

a flame

that can not rest

without your breath?

Who are you

to place my heart under

house arrest,

like a sealed love letter with no address?

The Poet

He reminds me of dudes from Jersey
with the fresh Timbs
shape-up
white tee.

He's in the subway squat
doing the ghetto bop
rocking his head
as he cools to some r and b.

And I want him to notice me.

A dark history
I recognize the tell
as my flesh surrenders
to his quiet spell.

Temptation,
the call of an enigma alone.

But he remains in his zone,
head down,
gripping an invisible poem.

I bet his thoughts feel like poetry.

And I want him to notice me.

Coup de Foudre

When we kiss

water rushes
a rugged isle

eroding your beaches
and soaking your shores

until plums grow
and vineyards sprout

where there used to be
only sand and salt.

Alchemy

On a night with two moons
and a perilous tide,
I caught my lover swimming
in my eyes.

Before I could save him
from the surging sea,
I emerged...

a rose in his window
a cloud in his tea.

Liner Notes

Mister Radio Man in his shiny Black jeep,
old school Chaka cut thumping,
slides up behind me,
asking kindly
for a dance.

Why can't I remember the day I melted before your charms?
Oh... was it way back in September when you held me in
your arms?

Drum break
is trapped in spine.
I'm arching my back,
wiggling my behind
and shaking my head
even after light turns green.

Mister Radio Man and his funk beat, keeps me grooving long
after he leaves.

Mister Radio Man rocks me to sleep,
with Sarah's voice,
dipped in whiskey notes
fall

like pennies
in a silk wishing well.

I do pretty well till after sundown...
Suppertime I'm feelin' sad,
But it really gets bad 'round midnight

I clench the pillow
like they are his shoulders,
inhale a cool
coconut
scent.
Chiaroscuro riffs
quiver.
I snuggle in her lament.

Mister Radio Man and his eloquent refrain, always seems to
numb t(his) pain.

In his milk crate of vinyl
there is a song for every mood.

He can be my break and break down,

bebopfunkgospelblues.

We take daily field trips
back down memory lane
He says:
ooh baby baby...
He asks:
can you stand the rain?

Mister Radio Man,
DJ to the hum drum
beat of life
keeps me spinning
on my A side
and My B(lue) side

leaving hand written notes
in every love song I hear
telling me how I feel,
touching me everywhere,
as if he was real

as if he was here.

By Surprise

There were no more words.
They'd been swallowed
by the sewers.
Tossed like
tumbleweed
down dark city
streets
and sprinkled over
barren fields.
There were
no
more
words.
And then you came a long
to write this poem.

In the In-Between

In the in between of things
a penis is a pacifier
to calm a fussy vagina
that cries for attention
and weeps for love.

In the in between of things
jisms make gospel rhythms
belly slaps
sound like
soul claps
and titties shake like tambourines

in the in between of things.

In the in between
there is laying of hands
and lying of flesh
and the cross
of spread legs
and breasts
bless
the sheets
(but not the freaks)

in the in between

women tithe
and men preach.

In the in between of things
a penis is a space ship
taking many trips
to sun moon and stars
women kneel
to make du'as
to their demi Gods
and anointed Kings
in the
in between
of things.

In the in

between
left and right

between
now and before

between

his story and gospel

between

sex and war.

Patria

(this too is a love poem, albeit a short one)

Freedom marches
freedom rides

chicken noodle soup
with a shuffle and a jive?

Did my heroes die in vain
so we could miss
our freedom train?

Black Maria

Black Maria,
you sadomasochistic whore.
You cheap, wretched,
five dollar
skank

scally wag
working the corner of 13th
and Malcolm X
showing your bony ass
to all the boys in the hood.

I see you

whispering
sweet nothings deep
in my brothers ear
Your voice
the shivering high-pitched
squeal of iron blades upbraiding steel

Are you being coy?
Or fucking with his mind?

I'm onto you.

Black Maria,
you told everyone
that it was an accident
but I know you singed
your own corneas
with the scorching end
of a fireplace tong
because you could no longer withstand
the sight of your reflection:
vulgar shit-faced gluttonous
      woman
with stale breath
and smutty   skin.

Black Maria,
you   aren't black.
You are   dirty
      white.

Black Maria,
I know that you've been nosing around my house.
I know you've been here, because
I smell that Charlie
in my seat cushions.

Let the record show that I never wear Charlie.

(it's cheap)

And besides,

you leave incriminating trails of virus in your path.

D(eath)isease drips from your

inner thighs.

(Will somebody get me some damn Lysol?)

Black Maria,

how come all the boys left your crib

straight faced

and scared straight?

How come no one wanted to talk about the music you played?

Or the Steel Reserve they drank?

Or the food they ate?

No one would say a thing,

but I know

I know that you lined them up

one   by   one,

and sodomized them senseless,

as they turned their heads,

to avoid your

rotten

snaggle-toothed

kisses.

You see, Black Maria,
No one wants to make love to you.
No one loves you.
You are my country's shame.
Some may like how you make them feel.
So they use you and
abuse you,
but no body loves you.
You don't love yourself.

Black Maria,
I know that you've been seeing a
therapist,
trying to reconcile your
privilege
with your abominable childhood.
I know you've been crouched
in fetal position
on his couch,
crying over letters,
as you discover the truth about
your immoral father.
You recount the nights
when you were frightened to sleep.

You knew those bare-foot
Black-faced
ghosts
who danced a jig
at the foot of your bed
would
      choke
          you
if you did.

Black Maria,
Apple Pie,
Kissed the boys
And made them cry.

I am the sister
who longs for her brother.
I am the daughter
without a daddy to spoil her.

Black Maria,
Apple Pie,
51 kisses
Made him die.

I am the lover
that never will never be a wife
because that bitch
seduced my soul mate
and put him away for life.

Arithmetic

I was once involved in this
affair
best described as love
on a diet.

I suckled on a bottom lip.
We made love in the quiet.

I ventured to the halfway point of
nothing
and a little more.

I let a two-faced
two-timing man
turn me into his part-time whore.

I snuggled in a
partial truth
(better known as a lie)

I drank the half-cup full
of kool aid
and was none the wise.

I fasted,

in his absence

from sun up to sun down,

praying that with the next moon

this man would come around.

He never did.

Perhaps he thought he was Dick Gregory,

helping me with

portion control.

He told me to be satisfied with

half a man.

Quit pining for a whole.

But he did love me,

with half his heart.

And here I am, supposed to be smart.

In retrospect, having so little to begin with

it must have been hard for him to divide that

by two...

I loved half a man once.

Does this mean I'm half the fool?

Half-Hearted Haiku

The next best thing to
Being under a man is
To be over him.

Silence

In an age where lips
are for talking,
and feet, for walking
there is a lot to be said for
silence.

Better yet,
in silence
there is a lot said.

Mmm hmmm.

Caged birds
forbidden escape
words
the tongue can't articulate
simply because
they have yet to form
in the crag of my throat.

Think of my silence
not as the absence of sound
but the presence of humility.

Two lips pursed
as they would be on the verge
of a kiss
to hum a pensive tune
to muffle a child's whimper
to curse not
to scorn

but be still
and possibly let the eyes and ears do their work
free of interruption.

Think of my silence
as
an abortion of seminal thought:
speak and it shall be. Don't
speak and it never was.
  This is the rule of empires
  civilization
  history
  and hallowed souls.

I know my silence upsets you
but please
don't resent the possibility of language.
These lips have yet to

mutter regret
to get upset
or to forget.
They have only kissed
and selfishly wished
for something more likely
to crumble in our hands.

We might never recover from those things
I could say.

My mouth contains
the spoils of war
the vitriol
and the sincerity.
All that you are
all that you were to me.
And for now
inside
the two enemies
may as well be friends.

Soul Food

Wait 'til you taste my red velvet cake

candied peaches

pecan pie.

Have some raisin

cinnamon bread.

Baby, savor my luscious spread

The Love Cup

He wet both lips,
wine spilled on his chin.
Eyes closed
he exhaled.
His nose broke the brim.

He surrendered
dizzy
and no longer sober.

He drank from my cup
until love ran over.

The Recondite Dream

Uncover me
as if this sheet
were a poem of one hundred lines
and astounding geometric cadence.

Insert your meaning
in between my own.

Unravel me
like unpunctuated language
that slips from the tongue
and shatters at your ankles.

Discolor me
with scratch marks
as you pierce these ephemeral allusions
with the presumptuous and concrete.

Devour me like
a su'ra. Then
close your eyes.

God is Love.

Commit me to memory,
let the opening stain your blood, and then
read me. Again
as I grow inside of you.

Know me
like you would know a forgotten language,
discovered after a thousand years.

Speak me,
and let me wilt against your desk top
burning pages,
igniting everything around you,
including your Id.

Dream of me
And of that one line unforgettable.
" ... "

At dawn my ashes tell no secret.

Gravity

(in memory of Virginia L. Faines)

How shall we breathe
when clouds empty?
When the world is still
without wind or rain.
How shall we stand
without gravity?
When time is still
how shall seasons change?

When She left
time followed in her path.
The seconds fled
to a place in the sky.
Air stopped flowing.
Buds stopped growing.
Birds abstained
from fruit and flight.

Now we yearn for the wisdom of yesterday
for a porch of laughter and
children at play.
When will we be able to taste our tears?

When will the seconds return to outnumber the years?

We seek love in the flesh of things
but it is neither here nor there
nor in the in-between.
But in the force at the center of a family bond
such that when our Matriarch leaves
we remain strong.

We find Her love in the margins of our pages,
in our nightly prayers,
in the pulse of our days.
We'll learn that love outlasts dust
time and space,
and that Queens depart,
but leave their grace.

And the Earth will one day move again
first slow, and then a quicker spin.
And there will be wind and the sweetest rain
though maybe, always, there will be pain.

And our Matriarch's love shall course through our veins.
And even the seasons shall find strength to change.

Sade-Sati

I know I have changed

By the way

My fingers   hug   the barrel

The orbit of   my wrist

The   weight

      Of my hand

And the way this ink

      Bleeds

Through the paper.

Jones

He carries blacks and blues
In the grooves of his hands.
He is the preacher
And the orisha,
Spinning psalms like pulsars
Sermoning his parishioners into fugue.
He strums the strings that make yonis sing,
He is a macabre epiphany,
The murky line
Between heaven and sea,
Pillar of song
Purveyor of sex
Dionysus...
With a man-complex.

Bucket List

I want to ruin

a man

so good

he thanks me

Killer Jo

Once upon a groovy theory
Lady scats with wicked fury
Notes are floating, enveloping
Me as I stop at the door.

Smoky club a rhythmic wonder
Thick percussion lures me under
Skirts are floating, men show boating
Between lust and love I'm tore.

Pipes blow circles toward the ceiling
Lady's singing rough with feeling
Body's shaking, hips gyrating
I place my heel upon the floor.

Through the murky scent of sexy
Still confused and heart perplexing
My arms sway as I sashay
Towards the stage where the band roars.

Handsome stranger touch me gentle
Two-steps smooth but temperamental
Wants me badly, but so sadly
My heart longs for that dark Moore.

Maybe wrong, but God forgive me
He brings out the fire within me
My string he's pulling, trumpet's lulling
Breathy blows like chocolate poured.

Lover's past a kindling secret
In the struggle, I proved weakest
Long roads traveled, sheets unraveled
'Til I cried out, "Never more".

Just his presence makes me quiver
Sparks across the dance floor slither
Drummer's tapping, he is rapping
Melodies so passion bore.

His eyes move through the masses
My heart melts as his glance passes
Starts again, at his sly grin
When the singer takes her four.

In a state of midnight madness
He appears just like black magic
Potent potion, I can't hold it
He twirls me across the floor.

Diamonds falling from the skies
Jazzy darkness and moonlight waltzes
Yet I fear the many years
Of a smooth talking Killer Jo.

Tawny night in shining armor
Felt hat tilted, no ones sharper
He dips me slow; he's my cocoa
He's like fine wine sipped on the shore.

But soon, the summer waves are crashing
Jolting us apart, a thrashing
Stroke of pain, the joy's away
And evil seeps into the door.

My graceful knight in shining armor
Glory lost can stand no longer
Hellish shooting, folks pursuing
Escape from the jealous gore.

A slow lament to croon so gently
Wicked love sweeps his stage empty
Am I to blame for acts insane
His body but a tragic lore?

Love is lost, and love is wicked

Sweet romance has made me sicker

Lust profane, a love in vain

And I will still tell him never more.

Upon the floor, my tears are sinning

Shouts to God of me repenting

I can't bear the grave despair

Slave to a love I don't adore.

I face the ground.

Oh, never more

A breath? Oh bless thy tenderly

This man is my serenity

My hand, his heart, we'll never part

He resurrects from the vile floor.

Oh my dark Moore,

Thy is a warrior

To steal his lady from unheard horrors.

A kiss dissolves, and he resolves,

That I should bear it never more.

Tragic hero, arise from seas

I'm praising God on blue black knees

Oh but it seems, this is my dreams

Exotic fantasies, so pure?

But into night we ride away
A 1960 Chevrolet
Road with secrets, even deeper
Than the roots of Sycamore.

The be-bops back, the funk remains
His trumpet playing fills my veins
Though evil sleeps and maybe seeks
Me, Desdemona with her Moore.

The night I laid, the night I prayed
The trumpets played, the dancers swayed
He changed my life, entwined with strife
With his caresses, his amore

And still he wishes never more.
And still he whispers never more.

Autumnal Seduction

They are the living and breathing colonnades,
the courtesans,
who stalk the walks and the glades.

A tease to the wandering eye that dares
to glimpse the azure sky where they bare

a supple shoulder, a crescent chin,
wild hair that furrows the succulent wind.

Their figures shrouded and lushly stowed
in the folds of gilded perfumed robes.

And once cold lips have coaxed the skin,
they slip out of those sanguine leaves of sin.

Slowly,
for this, a courtesan knows
to tempt is to bloom;
to surrender, expose.

A Letter to My Soul Mate

At the end of a love affair
I gave
them all
parting gifts.

Nothing fancy,
just
A small piece of sanity,
or a slither of calm,
and my smile
which is not nearly as wide as it
was
in my early twenties.

Tokens of
affection,
pride,
ego,
attitude.

I even gifted
some of the self-control
that makes me not call you
at awkward hours

or say too much over dinner
and panic every time you leave.

I gave
comb fulls of my
hair
my derriere
the glisten on my lips
and some of the love
that I had saved
for me.
I have given

my voice,
which is why
sometimes
when you hold me close
I have nothing to say.

A piece
of my
mind.

A piece
of my
peace.

Sometimes, in the absence of them
I gave me.
to be fair.

I wanted to be
in love
or to at least walk
the periphery...

And now that
you have arrived
I must take inventory
of how much of me
there is left
to love
you.

Perhaps if we split,
you will give me a parting gift too.

Made in the USA
Middletown, DE
11 March 2016